No movement comes from goose or cow or sheep
and farmyard sounds are muffled by the rain,
and when you think that everyone's asleep
the Bantam of the Opera sings again.

ototoooototototto

THE VERY WORST
OF
SIMON DREW

THE HOUND
OF THE BASKETBALLS

'golf is a good walk ruined'
mark twain

THE VERY WORST
OF
SIMON DREW

because a bird has no placenta
eggs is how this world they enter

ANTIQUE COLLECTORS' CLUB

I never travel without my
diary.   One should always
have something sensational
to read in the train.

oscar wilde

to
Caroline
and to Diana
who made all these books happen

©1999 Simon Drew
World copyright reserved

ISBN 1 85149 331 X

British Library Cataloguing-in-Publication Data
A catalogue record for this book is available from the British Library

Published and printed in England by the Antique Collectors' Club Ltd., Woodbridge, Suffolk

dali havidson

A french philosophical feline
supported a sink full of jam.
This strange aberration
had one explanation:
"I sink and so therefore I am."

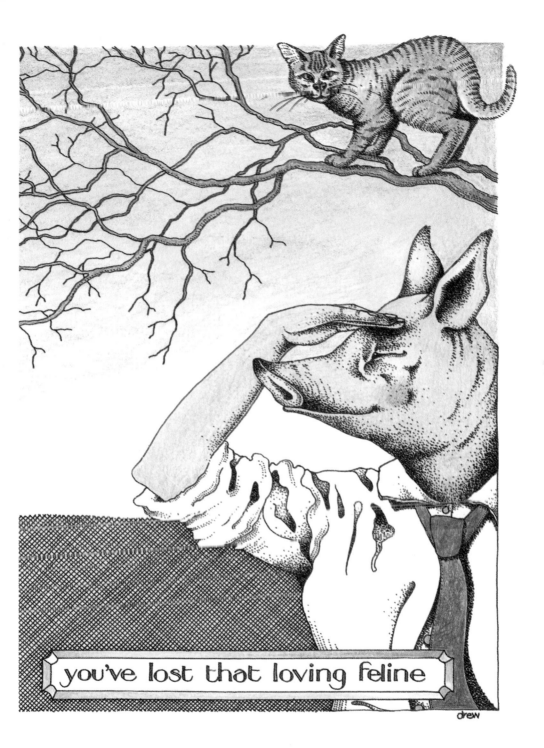

you've lost that loving feline

a slug in a salad is rather fright;
a fly in your tea is a miserable sight;
but one of the things that I utterly hate
is finding a hare on the side of my plate.

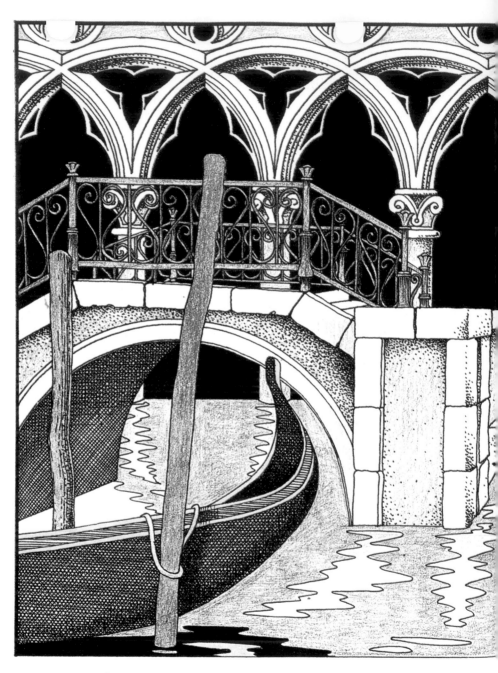

great mistakes of history:

the spotted doge of Venice

Cedric
was always
on his mobile fawn

PUFFIN

'I sometimes think that God,
in creating man,
somewhat overestimated his ability.'

oscar wilde

Corgi and Bess

I spy with my little eye
something beginning with 'O'

don't know

one pig

the truth about the road hog

however hard you hunt,
if pigs are in the front....
I'll bet you a fiver
there's a back sheep driver.

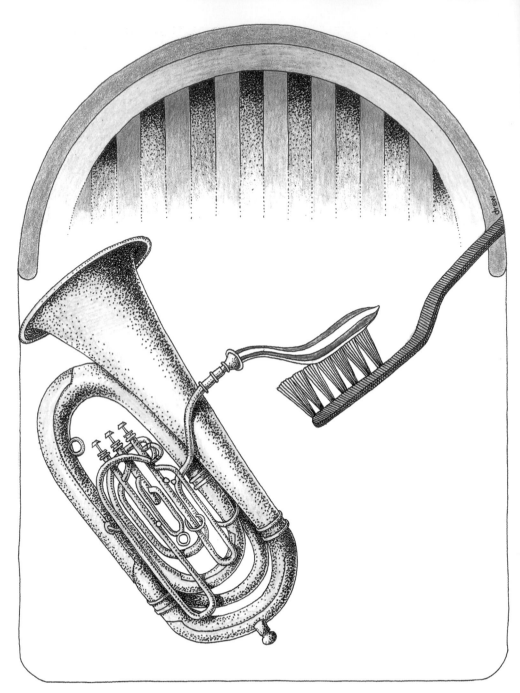

tuba toothpaste

GERSHWIN'S

RAT'S

BODY IN BLUE

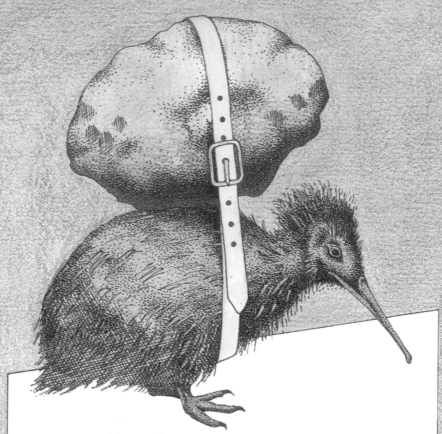

a flightless bird called Faith
began to carry boulders:
for years she took these weights
strapped between her shoulders;
and as you might expect
the sweat poured like a fountain,
but only time will tell
if Faith can move a mountain.

drew

poultry in motion

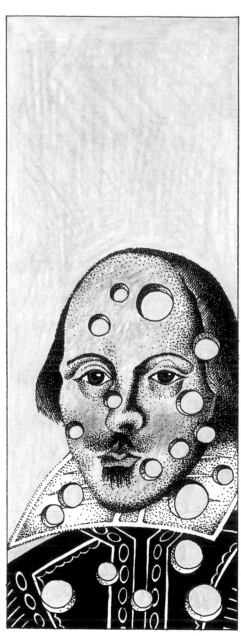 

shakespeare
with holes

no holes bard

last mango in Paris

only dull people
are bright at breakfast.

oscar wilde

origins of phrases:

still life in the old dog yet...

wolf gang mows art

A PIG'S TALE

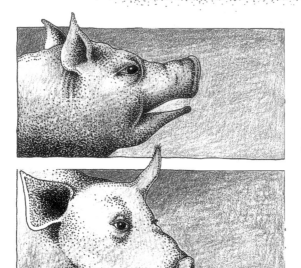

what do we
want ?

procrastination

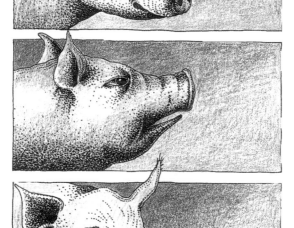

when do we
want it ?

next week

Magrittes
I've had a few
but then again, too few to mention.

SHEEP
DIP

jimi hen drinks

There aint nothing like a Dane

39

While walking through some farmyard pens,
past ploughs with rusty blades,

amongst the turkeys, geese and hens,
he found the three of spades.

Le déjeuner sur l'herbe avec deux canards

BASIC TRAINING

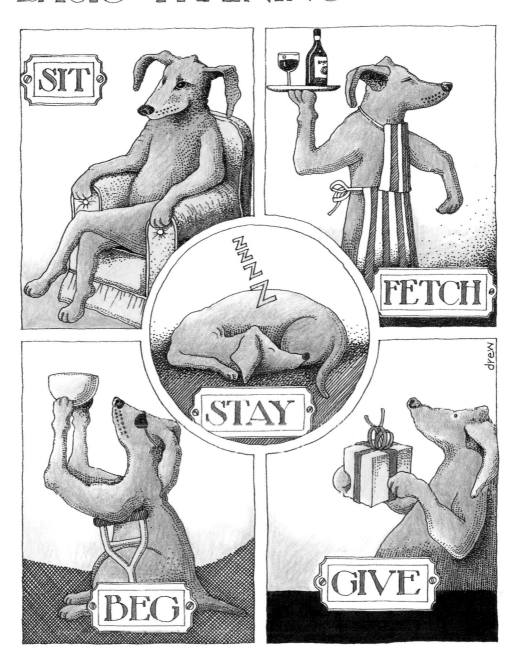

drew

newts in white satin

and there he stood....
tall duck and handsome

46

Hell and Dalmatian

47

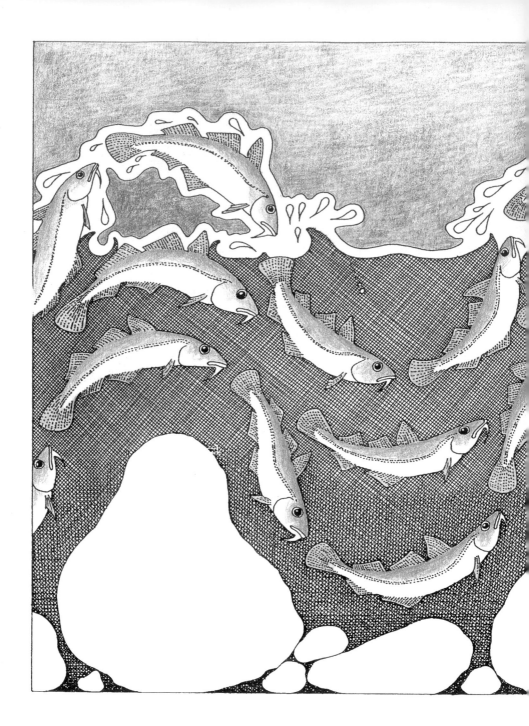

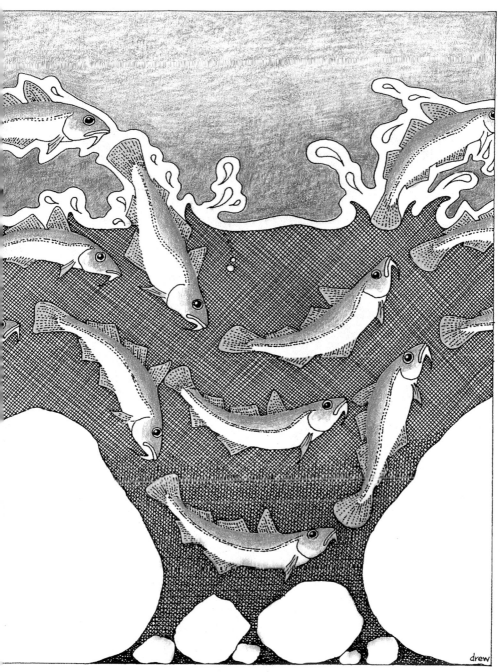

cod moving in a mysterious way

elephants gerald

tequila mocking bird

sea shark minor prelude

AQUARIUS
(the waterbearer) jan 20 to feb 18

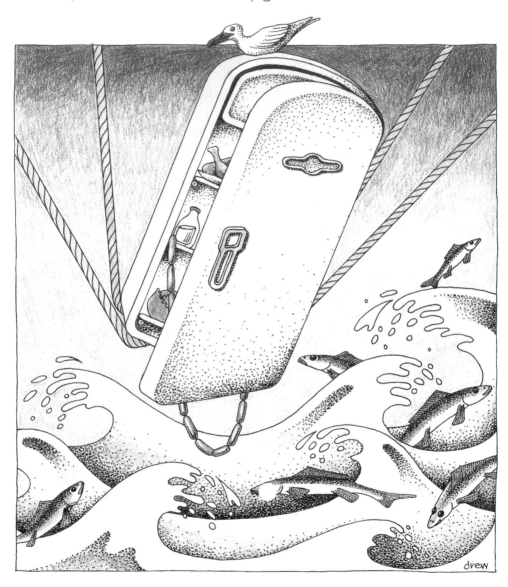

fridge
over troubled water

a cats 22 situation

BIRD DROPPING

SEMAPHORE EXPLAINED

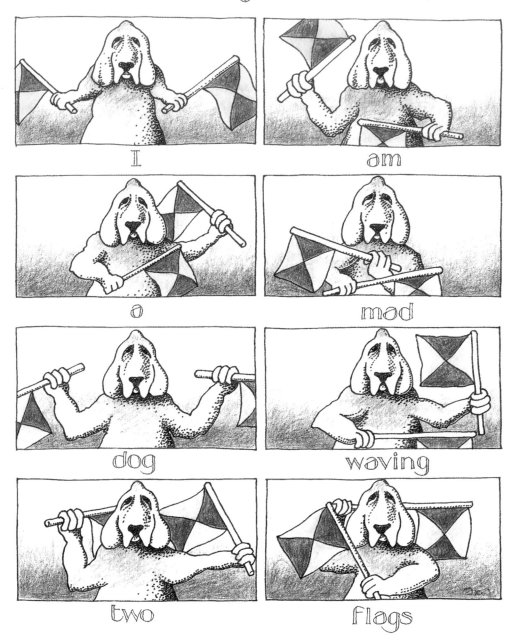

I am

a mad

dog waving

two flags

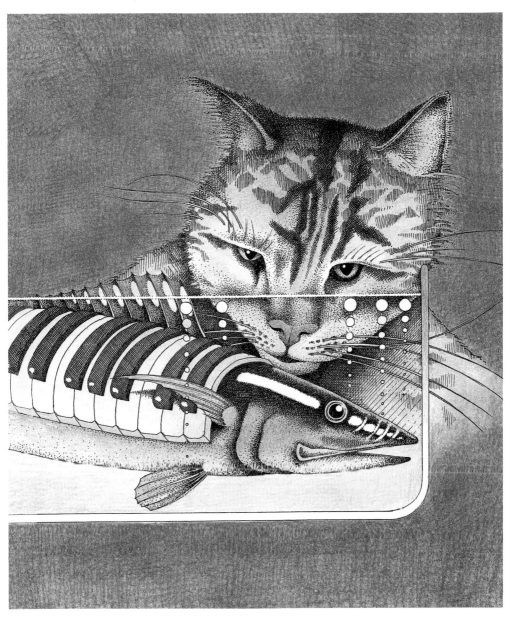

cat with piano tuna

'... frankly, my dear, I don't give Adam.'

pope springs eternal